Italian Quickies Cookbook
© Mel Alafaci 2023

First printed December 2023 by Ingram Spark

All rights reserved. Except as permitted under the Australian Copyright Act 1968 (for example, a fair dealing for the purposes of study, research, criticism or review), no part of this book may be reproduced, stored in a retrieval system, communicated or transmitted in any form or by any means without prior written permission.

Creator: Mel Alafaci (Author)
Title: Italian Quickies Cookbook
ISBN: 9780645808469 (Paperback)
Subjects: Cook Book

Typesetting by Chloe Reynolds - Social Chloe

Chef Mel is taking on the WORLD!

With a smile that can light up a room, Chef Mel Alafaci has become a globally recognised chef and food educator. Her recent success in the USA means she's Australia's hottest rising culinary personality. Born in Zimbabwe, Chef Mel lived in South Africa before moving to Australia and starting her reign in the global foodie market.

She has an unwavering passion for cooking, eating, and teaching. And her intoxicating enthusiasm, authenticity, and unique culinary lingo will have you hungry to flex your muscles in the kitchen. Chef Mel is brilliant at adding humour, shortcuts, tricks, and hacks to all those tedious tasks, as well as making the scary ones simple and easy to accomplish.

CHEF MEL THE HAPPY CHEF | @CHEFMEL_HAPPYCHEF | WWW.CHEFMEL.ME

ABOUT MEL

WILD ABOUT FOOD!

Mel Alafaci has been passionate about food her whole life. She's the founder of Vanilla Zulu Cooking School, one of Australia's leading cooking schools, and has more than 28 years of professional cooking experience.

People battle to say her surname... so to make it easy she calls herself CHEF MEL.

Foreword

I am so excited to share my incredible Italian QUICKIES Cookbook with you. I promise my methods are easy and reliable. These are some of my favourite recipes, I know there are so many other Italian recipes, but here is a collection of my personal favourites.

I am very passionate about Italian Cuisine.
I have been fortunate enough to travel extensively in Italy, and I also married into an Italian family, so my recipes are very authentic and approved.

You will be inspired, up-skilled, and unstoppable in the kitchen, and best of all, we will make delicious discoveries in your kitchen together.

This cookbook is designed to provide inspiration and creativity and build confidence, and these are my tried and trusted collection of Italian recipes, perfected through generations.

Experiment with friends and family, and make time for practice so that you can fix any mistakes you still may be making.
I also encourage you to join me on socials so that if you ever need any help, I'm a message away.

Chef Mel

"The trouble with eating Italian food is that five or six days later, you're hungry again."
— George Miller

Recipes

Recipes

Pane, Burro e Pizza
Breads, Butters & Pizza

- 3 — Ciabatta (no-knead, stretch & fold dough)
- 4 — Salt and Rosemary Focaccia
- 6 — Grissini Sticks
- 7 — Whipped Porcini or Truffle Butter
- 9 — Authentic Pizza

Antipasti
Starters

- 12 — Porcini Arancini
- 13 — Prosciutto & Goats Cheese with Roasted Pear & Fig Balsamic
- 15 — Rustic Chicken Liver Pate with Crostini
- 16 — Beef Carpaccio

Insalate
Salads

- 19 — Pear, Rocket & Parmesan Salad
- 21 — Caprese Salad

Recipes

Primi
Pastas & Risottos & More

23	Basic Pasta Recipe
25	Making Ravioli with a Ravioli Tray, or Free Cut, or Roller
26	Ravishing Roasted Sweet Potato & Speck Ravioli with Burnt Sage Butter
29	Ravishing Roasted Spinach & Ricotta Ravioli with Burnt Sage & Pine Nut Butter
31	Easy Carbonara
33	Change your Life Bolognaise
35	Mushroom Patè Pasta
37	House-made Ricotta
37	Ricotta & Walnut Pasta Filling
38	Marinated Vegetables
40	Spring Pea pasta
41	Pangritata (Crispy Breadcrumbs for Pasta)
43	Easy Risotto's

Salse
Sauces

45	Easy Cheesy Sauce
46	Truffle or Porcini Cream Sauce
47	Sexy Lemon Pepper Mayonnaise
48	Sugo Sauce
49	Sugo Sauce with Roasted Capsicum
51	Sicilian Caponata Sauce
53	Bacon & Porcini Mushroom Sauce

Recipes

Secondi
Mains

- 56 — Beautiful Beef Ragu
- 57 — Rustic Italian Gnocchi with burnt sage butter & pancetta bark
- 58 — Scallopini with Lemon Caper Sauce
- 59 — Involtini De Melanzane
- 60 — Chicken Involtini
- 62 — Epic Meatballs in Sugo Sauce
- 63 — Glam Lasagne
- 66 — Crab & Prawn Lasagne
- 68 — Polenta Bake with Italian Sausage

Dolci
Desserts

- 70 — Cannoli
- 72 — Gelato
- 73 — Vanilla Semi-Freddo
- 74 — Easy Vanilla Panna Cotta
- 75 — Chef Mel's Panna Cotta Variations
- 77 — Pear & Ricotta Tarts
- 79 — Death by Chocolate Tiramisu
- 81 — Nonna's Sponge Cake
- 82 — Almond Biscuits
- 84 — Raisin & Nut Biscotti
- 86 — Limoncello

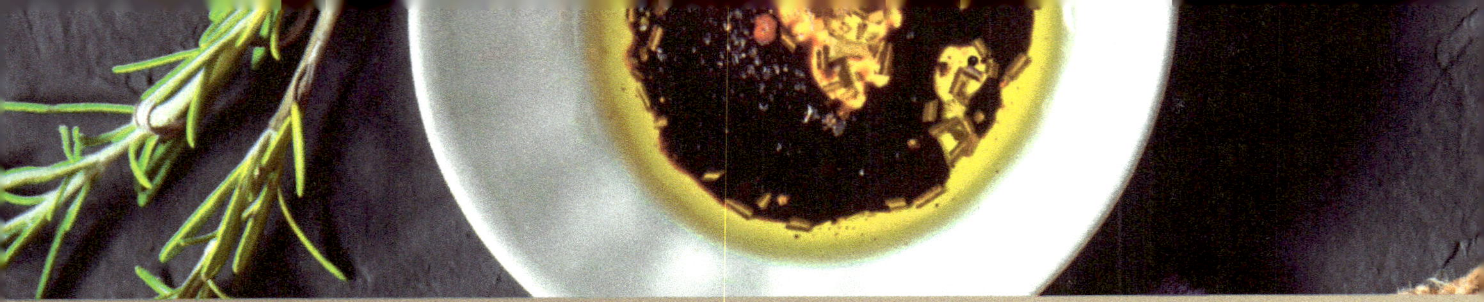

Pane, Burro e Pizza

Breads, Butters & Pizza

Ciabatta (No Knead Stretch & Fold Dough)

Ciabatta
(No Knead, High Hydration, Stretch & Fold Dough)

SERVINGS: 8-12

INGREDIENTS

350g baker's flour
1 heaped teaspoon of instant yeast
280ml hand hot water (not cold or swearword hot)
1 flat teaspoon salt
30ml/2 tablespoons olive oil
1 tablespoon chopped rosemary
1/4 cup chopped olives (optional)

METHOD

This is super easy; you are going to just love this dough.
Please watch my full demo on my YOUTUBE channel.

Add all the ingredients into a large bowl and use a strong spoon to bring it together. Once mixed nicely, it will look a lot wetter than a standard bread dough, cover with a wet cloth and then allow to prove for 10 minutes. After ten minutes, you should see some yeast bubble activity. Dip your hand in water from a tap or bowl, and then when your hand is wet, dig down along the side of the bowl under the dough and then scoop and stretch the dough to the top and centre.

Repeat this stretch and fold method about 8 times, turning the bowl as you go; keep wetting your hand so that the dough doesn't stick to you. Prove again for a further 10 minutes, repeat the stretch and fold and then prove and stretch and fold for a third and final time. The dough is now ready to be shaped, so turn it out onto a floured surface. It's a bit tricky to handle, but cut it into two smaller breads or leave it as one large one, depending on what you want and how long you have to cook this. Two smaller breads are faster than one large loaf.

Simply fold the dough over itself, shape it into an oblong or round and place it on a greased and floured baking tray. Sprinkle with about half a teaspoon of flour and then allow to prove for 10 more minutes in it's new shape. Bake, hot and fast, at about 190c for 15 minutes; remove from the oven, wet your hand and flick the crust with a sprinkle of water, and then bake further for approximately 5-8 minutes until nice and crunchy and brown. The water flicking helps create that spectacular crust we get on baguettes and artisan loaves; it's very cool to know how to do this. To test the bread, flick it with your fingers, it should sound hollow and should be gorgeous and brown.

Allow to cool and then cut, serve and enjoy!

Salt & Rosemary Focaccia

SERVINGS: 6-8

INGREDIENTS

DOUGH
- 450 g plain or baker's flour
- 2 teaspoons instant yeast
- 2 teaspoons sugar
- 320 ml lukewarm water,
- 1 teaspoon salt
- 30ml oil
- 2 teaspoons extra flour
- 2 tablespoons polenta
- Cooking spray to grease the baking tray

TOPPINGS
- 1/2 teaspoon black or other flake salt
- 1 tablespoon finely chopped Rosemary cut into a gravel
- 3 large lashings of extra virgin olive oil
- Olives for garnish if you like

METHOD

Add the yeast to the warm water, with the 2 teaspoons extra flour and sugar, stir and set aside for about 10 minutes until foamy. Mix this liquid with the flour, salt and oil until it forms a smooth dough. Place on a floured surface and knead until the dough is smooth and pliable. Use your mixer and a dough hook if you aren't doing this by hand, about 5-7 minutes at least!

Now place the dough into a greased bowl and, cover it with a clean wet cloth, and allow to prove for about 15 minutes or until doubled in size. Grease a baking tray with the cooking spray and then add the polenta shake to coat the tray. Remove the dough ball from the covered bowl and place it on the polenta baking tray. Put some oil on your palms and then spread the dough over the polenta to each end of the baking tray. Make deep holes (Nona's fingerprints) using your fingertips to poke the dough. Garnish with the sexy black salt flakes, rosemary gravel and oil. Now allow to prove for a second time for about 10 minutes in its shape, and then bake in a pre-heated oven of 180 c for about 15 minutes until golden.

TO SERVE

TO SERVE: Pour 2 tablespoons of extra virgin olive oil onto a saucer or side plate, and pour a tablespoon of balsamic vinegar in the middle of the plate.

Olive Oil & Balsamic Dipping Sauce for Bread

Grissini Sticks

SERVINGS: 6-8

INGREDIENTS

225 g baker's flour
1 teaspoon instant yeast
160 ml lukewarm water,
1 teaspoon extra flour
1 teaspoon sugar
15 ml oil
1/2 teaspoon salt

METHOD

Add the yeast to the warm water, with the extra teaspoon of flour and sugar, stir and set aside for about 10 minutes until foamy. Now mix this liquid with the flour, salt, and oil and bring it together until it forms a smooth dough. Place on a floured surface and knead until the dough is smooth and pliable. Use your mixer and a dough hook if you aren't doing this by hand, about 5 minutes at least!

Now place the dough into a greased bowl and, cover it with a clean wet cloth, and allow to prove for about 15 minutes or until doubled in size.

Remove from the bowl and shape on a floured surface into long cigar cylinders. Rolling with your hands to stretch it into a long cigar.
Now allow to prove for a second time for about 10 minutes in its shape, and then bake in a pre-heated oven of 180 c for about 15 minutes until golden. Keep an eye on them to know your oven - you want them fully golden, so they'll be crispy. If they are still soft when cooled, they need a couple more minutes.

NOTE
You can be very cheffy by rolling your raw cigar dough cylinders in black salt, sesame seeds, cracked pepper or fresh, chopped rosemary to add a little bling!

Whipped Porcini or Truffle Butter

SERVINGS: 12-16

INGREDIENTS

250g salted butter
3 tablespoons dried mushroom powder (blend dehydrated mushrooms in a food processor) or truffles, grated or bought as a paste.

METHOD

Grate the butter into a large bowl of a stand mixer. Start on a low speed and whip the butter using a balloon whisk. You must stop the machine and scrape the sides down when the butter becomes a yellow paste. This will take about 3-5 minutes. Now, put the machine on a faster speed and allow the butter to 'whip' and go nearly white; scrape down the side of the bowl occasionally as required. The whole process will take at least 15 minutes, but I promise it's worth it. Once it is whipped and white, add the porcini mushroom powder OR the shaved/grated truffles. Mix until well combined and then place on the middle of a large piece of baking paper.

Arrange the whipped butter down the centre and then gather the edges of the paper and manipulate the butter into a sausage or a cylinder. Wrap and seal by either twisting the ends of the paper or using elastic bands to tie. You can then pop it in the fridge or freezer until you need to use it, and cut off discs using a hot knife. You can also pop this in an airtight container and make 'ice cream scoops' placed in a gorgeous bowl if you prefer. I always make you make extra because this is wonderful to have in the freezer or fridge for the next time you need it.

PERFECT FOR SERVING WITH BREAD, STEAKS, CHICKEN OR ROASTED VEGETABLES.

Authentic Pizza

Authentic Pizza

SERVINGS: 6-8

INGREDIENTS

DOUGH	PIZZA SAUCE
1kg "OO" or bakers flour	3 tablespoons olive oil, to fry
650ml cold water	1 brown onion, finely chopped
15g salt	2 cloves garlic
2g instant yeast	1 tablespoon freshly chopped marjoram or oregano
	(or use 1 teaspoon dried)
TO HANDLE DOUGH AND ROLL	500ml tomato passata
Semolina, about 1 cup	salt and pepper to season
	1 fresh chilli optional

METHOD

This is the best-ever pizza base recipe. It is easy and reliable and gives a very authentic result. If you are doing this in your oven at home, I recommend a pizza stone and I also recommend pre-heating it at at least 280 C for 20-30 minutes. Remember, in the pizza ovens in restaurants they get their base heat of the stone to upwards of 320 C...so hot is essential for an authentic puff and browning of the base for a good flavour and crunch.

Fry the onions and the garlic in the oil until just soft. Now add the tomato passata/puree, herbs and the seasoning and cook through. Adjust seasonings. Allow to cool and then store in the fridge. Best pizza sauce but also a fantastic sauce for all sorts of pasta and mains.

To make the dough, add all these ingredients together, except for the semolina, and knead for 5-8 minutes with a stand mixer and dough hook. Divide into four or six dough balls and cover with a wet cloth or wrap, and then store in the fridge for at least 12 hours or overnight. If the dough is sticky, add flour to the work surface, and your hands, this will make them less stressful to handle.

Hand stretch the dough ball using your semolina on the bench. the easiest way to do this is to start by pressing the dough thinner from the middle to the outside, leaving a lovely thick edge. Turn the dough and keep working from the middle to the outside. Now top with sauce using a metal spoon; you can thin your dough a little using the back of the spoon, but KEEP THAT BORDER nice and thick. Top with your favourite ingredients, and then bake hot and fast, turning as you go, until you have a brown and crunchy base. A pizza oven base should be really hot, so ensure you have pre-heated it for at least half an hour.

There are three official variants of Neapolitan pizza:
PIZZA MARINARA: Topped with tomato, garlic, oregano, and extra-virgin olive oil.
PIZZA MARGHERITA: Topped with tomato, fresh sliced mozzarella, fresh basil, and extra-virgin olive oil.
PIZZA MARGHERITA EXTRA: Topped with tomato, sliced mozzarella di Bufala, fresh basil, and extra-virgin olive oil.

Antipasti

Starters

Porcini Arancini

Porcini Arancini

SERVINGS: 4-6

INGREDIENTS

Olive oil
1 onion, finely chopped
2 cloves garlic, finely chopped
1 cup Arborio rice
1 tablespoon parsley, chopped
1 tablespoon sage, chopped
80ml white wine (optional)
750ml hot mushroom, vegetable or chicken stock (depends on the size of the pot)
(Don't make the stock too strong as it reduces and will leave you with salty rice!)
80g grated Parmesan or pecorino
1/2 cup fresh porcini mushrooms, chopped or 2T rehydrated porcini
1 egg and 1/2 cup breadcrumbs to dry out and bind the rice
Bocconcini
Breadcrumbs or rice crumbs
Vegetable or Rice Bran oil for frying

METHOD

Heat 50ml olive oil. Add the onion and garlic and cook, stirring, over gentle heat. Add the rice and ensure that all grains are coated with the oil. Add the mushrooms, then whilst stirring, add the wine, and when absorbed, start adding the hot stock, 1 cup at a time, allowing it to be absorbed before more is added. Stir the parsley, sage and Parmesan, add the breadcrumbs and the egg through then place in the refrigerator to cool. The risotto should be quite dry with the rice cooked through.

Heat the oil for frying. Roll the risotto into firm and well-compacted balls, about a tablespoon in size. Create a hole and, place a small piece of bocconcini in the middle and cover with the risotto. Roll in breadcrumbs. Refrigerate to set, about 10 minutes or you can make these the day before if you want to! Fry in the oil until golden brown. Drain on absorbent paper.
IF THE BALLS ARE FALLING APART IN THE OIL, YOU HAVE NOT COMPACTED THEM ENOUGH…rather than panic or give up, make an egg wash. Coat the crumbed balls in the egg wash and more crumbs, and then they should be okay, as the egg will create a protective layer!

TO SERVE
Arrange Arancini balls on serving dishes and serve with a sauce of your choice.

Prosciutto & Goats Cheese with Roasted Pear & Fig Balsamic

SERVINGS: AS REQUIRED

INGREDIENTS

2 slices prosciutto per person
1 tablespoon goats cheese per person
micro-herbs or chopped parsley to garnish/rocket sprigs
2-3 pears/apples/quince sliced and roasted in the oven (for about 20-25 minutes until they form 'chips')

METHOD

Place the sliced pears/apples/quince on a greased baking tray and then bake for about 20-25 minutes until dried and crisp. They will dehydrate slightly and will have so much more flavour like this.

Place the prosciutto on the plate and top with the roasted fruit. Now roll the goats cheese into balls, and garnish with the chopped herbs as per the photo, and then serve with rocket and some of the fig balsamic!

Rustic Chicken Liver Pate with Crostini

Rustic Chicken Liver Pate with Crostini

SERVINGS: 8-12

INGREDIENTS

100 g cold smoked bacon/speck chopped
2 tablespoons butter
500 g duck/chicken livers
1 medium onion sliced
2 cloves garlic crushed
100 ml chicken stock
50 ml marsala or sherry(optional)
1 teaspoon fresh thyme or sage
120 ml cream

METHOD

Trim the livers if necessary, rinse and pat dry.
Heat the frying pan with the butter and fry the bacon until brown and crisp.
I know this looks like a lot of oil, but we need this for the livers and for flavour.
Add the onions and the garlic and allow to cook through. Now add livers, tarragon, and stock.

Allow it to cook through and almost dry out, then scrape the food to the side of the pan so that it is 'clean' and will heat up. Once hot, add the brandy, and when bubbling ignite, TAKE CARE, but the flame will only go upwards, so please avert your face!

Shake while flaming to release the alcohol, and then the flames will die out.
Add the cream and butter last. Season to taste and then allow to cool.
Place in blender and blend until smooth.
Place in ramekin dishes or other suitable dishes and top with extra virgin olive oil or melted butter if you are not serving the pate immediately.

Serve with crostini: thick, toasted slices of bread drizzled with olive oil and salt.

Beef Carpaccio

SERVINGS: 4-6

INGREDIENTS

200g trimmed beef fillet
Juice and zest of two lemons
Extra virgin oil to drizzle
Salt and freshly ground pepper
Shaved Parmesan or Pecorino cheese or even whipped goats cheese dollops
Roast beetroot and basil leaves

METHOD

Slice the beef fillets into thin medallions. You can partially freeze the fillet first to make it easier to slice. Place the medallions on a plastic chopping board (or similar) that has been brushed with olive oil. Place another plastic sheet on top and beat with a mallet until paper thin. Place the paper-thin slices of Carpaccio onto a large white plate. Drizzle with lemon juice and zest. Drizzle with oil. Season. Then garnish with the cheese and your choice of toppings.

You can also try this with capers, thinly sliced onions and anchovies if you dare! Or even fresh chilies.

Insalate

Salads

Pear, Rocket & Parmesan Salad

Pear, Rocket & Parmesan Salad

SERVINGS: 2

INGREDIENTS

SALAD

Rocket, 1 bunch or packet

2 x medium pears

60 g Parmesan cheese, shaved

2 tablespoons toasted walnuts or pine nuts

SIGNATURE VINAIGRETTE DRESSING

50ml White or Red Wine Vinegar

150ml Extra Virgin Olive Oil

1 Teaspoon Mustard

Pinch Salt and Pepper

1/4 teaspoon honey or maple

1 teaspoon chopped fresh

herbs, either parsley, basil or sweet marjoram

METHOD

Thinly slice or julienne the pears.

Add all ingredients to a large bowl and toss to combine.

Just before serving, add the dressing and combine gently.

There is enough dressing for you to keep for next time.

SIGNATURE VINAIGRETTE DRESSING

This delightful dressing is very adaptable; use whatever you have in the pantry!

This will keep for up to one month in the fridge.

Caprese Salad

SERVINGS: 2-4

INGREDIENTS

2-3 ripe truss or Roma tomatoes, thickly sliced
Lots of fresh basil leaves
6-8 slices fior de latte, bocconcini or mozarella
Salt and pepper to season
Balsamic vinegar to drizzle
Extra virgin olive oil to drizzle

METHOD

This is a very simple combination of salad that doesn't really need a method.
You can simply layer or arrange the tomato slices and cheese with the basil leaves.
Season just before you serve, and then drizzle with extra virgin olive oil and beautiful balsamic vinegar or glaze.

Primi

Pastas & Risottos & More

Basic Pasta Recipe

SERVINGS: 2-3

INGREDIENTS

300g '00' flour
3 large eggs
10ml water, depending on the size of the egg
you will need less if you use an XL or Jumbo egg

METHOD

Simply combine all the ingredients together in a large bowl using a strong spoon. Once you have incorporated all of the moist ingredients into the flour, place the dough onto a floured surface, dust your hands with flour, and then knead, adding flour the minute the dough sticks to your hands. It should eventually go nice and smooth and elastic and pliable. Place in a lightly greased bowl under a wet cloth or cover and rest for about 20 minutes in the fridge or on the bench.

It is now ready to either hand roll OR put through a pasta machine.
To get the dough ready to roll out nice and thin, divide the dough in half using a strong knife. Roll each piece into a rough rectangle, about 'earlobe' thick. It should then be able to go through your pasta roller on the widest setting. Always dust with flour to prevent the dough from sticking back to itself. Continue until you reach the desired thickness, and then use a knife or the pasta machine to cut into the pasta shape you require. You can also use this long sheet to make your own lasagna sheets, cannelloni and many more.

You can use it straight away or allow it to dry by hanging over the back of a chair or a pasta drying rack.

Ravioli

Making Ravioli with a Ravioli Tray, or Free Cut, or Roller

INGREDIENTS

INGREDIENTS

Fresh pasta dough as per the basic pasta recipe page 23

Your choice of ravioli filling, e.g. cheese, spinach, meat, etc.)

Flour (for dusting)

EQUIPMENT

Ravioli tray or ravioli roller

Rolling pin/pasta machine

Pastry brush and some egg wash (egg beaten with 100ml water)

Sharp paring knife or ravioli cutter

METHOD

I have done a tutorial video on my YouTube Channel called Chef Mel The Happy Chef for this, so please watch it; it's easy when you know how! Head to Chef Mel's Quick and Easy Pasta video

Cut the 300g pasta dough ball into two. Press the smaller dough balls down into a rough rectangle, using the palm of your hand and a rolling pin to shape the dough. Once it is in a rough rectangle shape, roll it with a rolling pin until it is a bit thinner, but keep the rectangle shape if you are using a pasta machine. Put the pasta machine on the widest setting and then roll through. Continue until the pasta is thin enough so when you draw a love heart in flour on the bench and put your pasta dough over the flour heart, you can clearly read the heart. On a clean, floured surface, roll out the pasta dough.

If you are doing the ravioli by hand, Pipe or spoon dollops of the prepared filling about 5cm apart, leaving a little border around each one and then top with a sheet of fresh pasta. Press down around each round of filling, and then use your sharp knife or roller cutter to make little squares.

OR Prep the ravioli tray by flouring it with LOTS of flour.: Lay one sheet of pasta over the ravioli tray, making sure it fits over the sides of the tray; use your sharp knife to cut to fit. Brush the base pasta sheet with a little egg wash to cover the entire surface.

Use a teaspoon to spoon a small amount of your chosen filling into each well on the ravioli tray. Be careful not to overfill, as it might cause the ravioli to break during cooking. Top with another layer of pasta: Lay another sheet of pasta over the filled tray. Seal the ravioli: Press down firmly on the pasta, ensuring it sticks to the filling and the bottom layer of the pasta. This will help create a seal around each ravioli. Remove excess pasta: Run a rolling pin or a knife across the tray's surface, removing any excess pasta and creating individual ravioli pieces. Turn the tray over and give it a firm tap to release the ravioli; you can also push them out; take care not to tear them.

Cook the ravioli: Bring a large pot of salted water to a boil. Add the ravioli and cook according to the pasta dough's cooking time (usually 4-6 minutes for fresh ravioli).

Serve: Drain the ravioli and serve with your favourite sauce or toppings.

Ravishing Roasted Sweet Potato & Speck Ravioli with Burnt Sage Butter

SERVINGS: 4-6

INGREDIENTS

PASTA

300g 'OO' soft fine flour

3 large free-range eggs

5-10ml water (depends on the size of the eggs)

BURNT SAGE BUTTER SAUCE

100g salted butter

12-24 fresh sage leaves

EGG WASH

1 egg whisked with 30ml water

FILLING

2 cups roasted pumpkin or sweet potato, slightly mashed

1/2 cup fresh ricotta/or use parmesan grated (to taste)

½ cup finely diced and cooked speck/bacon bits

1 teaspoon freshly chopped garlic

Salt and pepper to season

1 teaspoon fresh oregano, basil and thyme

Freshly grated Parmesan or Pecorino

METHOD

PASTA

Place the flour, eggs and water in a bowl and mix with a large, strong spoon, stirring to bring everything together to form a rough ball. When you can form a rough ball, place it on a floured work surface and knead the dough until smooth. If your eggs are small, you may have to add another 5ml water, but bring the dough together for your hand first to see how wet the dough is.

Place to rest in a greased bowl and cover with a clean, wet cloth for at least 20 minutes before rolling as required.

FILLING

Mix together and use to stuff the ravioli as per the demo on the YouTube channel or as per the directions I gave on the previous how-to-make ravioli page …don't forget to use egg wash, or else your ravioli will unravel…and always cook in lots of boiling salted water when the ravioli rise to the surface they are done, about 6-8 minutes (if they are full of air bubbles they will rise sooner so always test one to make sure).

Brown 100g butter over low heat with fresh sage leaves, and use this gorgeous fragranced butter to drizzle and lift the flavour of the ravioli. Add lemon/lime zest for a flavour sensation.

BURNT SAGE BUTTER SAUCE

Simply brown 100g butter over a low heat with fresh sage leaves, and use this gorgeous fragranced butter to drizzle and lift the flavour of the ravioli.

Add lemon/lime zest for a flavour sensation. You can also use sugo or the roasted capsicum puree here.

HOW TO SERVE

Serve the gorgeous ravioli with the roasted capsicum sauce, the burnt butter sauce, and lots of grated Pecorino and live happily ever after.

Burnt Butter Sage Sauce

Ravishing Roasted Spinach & Ricotta Ravioli with Burnt Sage & Pine Nut Butter

SERVINGS: 4-6

INGREDIENTS

PASTA
- 300g "OO" soft fine flour
- 3 large free-range eggs
- 10ml water

EGG WASH
- 1 egg whisked with 30ml water

FILLING
- 150g baby or chopped spinach
- 300g fresh ricotta
- 60-70g Parmesan cheese finely grated
- 1 teaspoon freshly chopped garlic
- Salt and pepper to season
- 1 teaspoon fresh oregano or sage

METHOD

PASTA

Place the flour, eggs, and water in a bowl and mix with a large strong spoon, stirring to bring everything together to form a rough ball. When you can form a rough ball, place it on a floured work surface and knead the dough until smooth. Place to rest in a greased bowl and cover with a clean, wet cloth for at least 20 minutes before rolling as required.

FILLING

Simply mix together and use the wonderful filling to stuff the ravioli as per the previous recipe instructions… don't forget to use egg wash, or else your ravioli will unravel, and always cook in lots of boiling salted water. Cook the ravioli for about 6-8 minutes (if they are full of air bubbles, they will rise sooner, so always test one to make sure)

BURNT SAGE AND PINE NUT BUTTER

Simply brown 100g butter over low heat with about 12 fresh sage leaves and 2 tablespoons pine nuts and use this gorgeous fragranced butter to drizzle and lift the flavour of the ravioli. Add lemon zest for a flavour sensation.

TO SERVE

Serve the gorgeous ravioli with the roasted capsicum sauce and the burnt butter sauce, and live happily ever after!

Easy Carbonara

Easy Carbonara

SERVINGS: 4-6

INGREDIENTS

4-6 cloves garlic, crushed
2-3 rashers bacon or speck, diced
200-300g dried angel hair or spaghetti
4 eggs, beaten with 120 ml water
(reserved from the pasta cooking water)
4 tablespoons chopped parsley, chives, basil or sage - you choose!
4 tablespoons grated or shaved Parmesan or Pecorino
Salt and pepper to season

METHOD

Heat and grease the frying pan well; use a little oil just so it doesn't stick.

Place the diced bacon and the crushed or sliced garlic in the pan and let the bacon go crisp and brown and flavoursome. You want to render all the fat off; that is where the flavour is, after all.

Add the cooked spaghetti pasta, making sure you reserve 120ml of the pasta water.

Remove from pan from the heat and place on a heat proof surface. Get two chopsticks or a fork, and stir the hot liquid from the pasta water, little by little and very briskly, into the egg. Now add this egg and water to the pasta in the pan and stir through well. The residual heat will slowly thicken the egg as you stir and make a gorgeous, naturally thick sauce.

Once nice and thick, you can season it with the cheese and then serve it with cracked pepper.

Chef Mel's NOTE: Carbonara is easy, but if you have ever tried to make this before and the egg curdled, fear not. Try again; here, I have watered down the egg a little so that it's less sensitive.

Bellissimo!

Change your Life Bolognaise

Change your Life Bolognaise

SERVINGS: 4-6

INGREDIENTS

1kg premium beef mince
1 large onion finely sliced
3-6 cloves garlic
3 tablespoons fresh oregano/thyme/marjoram or use 1 teaspoon dried Italian herb mix
1 carrot finely diced or grated
1 celery stalk finely grated
1 pinch nutmeg (very important!)
80ml milk
3 tablespoons olive oil
2-3 teaspoons beef stock powder or 2 stock cubes
1 tin chopped tomatoes
1 jar passata (500-700ml)

METHOD

The first thing you should do is heat and grease a large pan until it is just about smoking hot. Now add the mince…we want the mince to sizzle when it hits the pan, and IT SHOULD SIZZLE nice and loud and sexy.

DO NOT STIR. I know you are worried about this burning, and you are also worried about lumps, but let the mince brown and seal on the first side you put down FIRST and let the pan heat up again, and THEN you can stir ever so slightly just to get some more mince onto the base of the pan. My favourite mince 'fluffer' is one of those cheap plastic-coated whisks you get at the supermarket that only have about 4 loops. If you don't have one of those, use a strong plastic spoon or egg flip to break down the mince.

Once the mince is brown and fragrant and sexy ALL BY ITSELF, then and only then do you add the finely chopped onion and garlic. There should be enough oil out of the mince that you have rendered off during your amazing sizzle-cooking of the mince at a nice high heat. If not, add the olive oil. You can stir as much as you like now, by the way; that mince is SEALED off. Now add the herbs, nutmeg, milk, stock powder, grated/diced carrot, and seasoning and stir through. Amazing colour, isn't it?

Finally, add the chopped tomatoes, vegetables, and passata, and you're practically done. Turn down the heat and let that all cook through, and then check the seasoning, and it's ready to serve. This way of cooking will not only save you time, BUT it will add valuable flavour and vibrant personality to your otherwise boring mince.

Serve with fresh al dente spaghetti, shaved parmesan, and lots of freshly chopped parsley. I also like to add some personality by serving this with the pangritata (sexy breadcrumbs), which you will find in this book.

Mushroom Patè Pasta

Mushroom Patè Pasta

SERVINGS: 4-6

INGREDIENTS

1 tin cannellini beans, drained
1 clove crushed garlic
1 cup mushrooms (tightly packed)
1 small shallot
Fresh thyme
1 tablespoon Porcini Mushroom Dust or mushroom stock cube
1 tablespoon grated Parmigiana Reggiano
1 x 300g prepared, cooked tagliatelle or similar pasta

METHOD

In a shallow fry pan, sauté shallot and garlic with a large splash of olive oil.

Add onion and continue to sauté until mushrooms are nice and golden.
Set aside and let cool before adding all other ingredients to a food processor to form a smooth, slightly dry paste. It should be the consistency of a pate.
You can now stir through your favourite cooked pasta.

Serve with Burnt Butter Sauce or a Creamy Sauce of 1 cup of cream brought to a boil, then add 4 tablespoons Parmesan, 1 heaped tablespoon Ricotta and a good healthy grating of fresh nutmeg.

Remember, this is a rich sauce so just toss the pasta through and let it kiss the sauce, lightly hugged in its velvety texture.

House-made Ricotta

House-made Ricotta

SERVINGS: 4

INGREDIENTS

1 liter full cream milk
60 ml lemon juice or white vinegar
1 teaspoon salt

METHOD

Bring the milk and the salt to the boil while stirring. Once little bubbles form, keep the heat on and add the vinegar or lemon juice; stir gently, and you will see the milk splitting into curds and whey.

Remove from heat, then pour into a clean cloth set in a colander and squeeze out the remaining liquid. Cool and then use or store for up to four days in the refrigerator.
You can add lemon zest or black pepper to make this a bit more gorgeous and delicious.

Ricotta & Walnut Pasta Filling

SERVINGS: 4-6

INGREDIENTS

2 cups of Ricotta
(see previous recipe to make your own)
1 tablespoon lemon zest
1 cup chopped walnuts
1 cup of shredded cheese (Parmesan or Pecorino)
Salt and pepper
*Extra tip: you can add chopped ham or crispy small-diced bacon

METHOD

Mix all ingredients in a bowl until smooth, use to fill pasta like ravioli, and tortellini or simply stir through freshly cooked tagliatelle or spaghetti pasta. You could also use this to fill involtini,

Marinated Vegetables

SERVINGS: 8-12

INGREDIENTS

VEGETABLES

1 large eggplant sliced and diced
2 red capsicums/peppers, diced
1 cup button mushrooms
2 large carrots, peeled and diced
12 garlic cloves, whole
olive oil to drizzle
salt and pepper to season

MARINADE

150ml White or Red Wine Vinegar
150ml Extra Virgin Olive Oil
1 teaspoon grainy mustard
Pinch Salt and Pepper
2 teaspoons honey or maple, or sugar
1 tablespoon chopped fresh herbs,
either parsley, basil or sweet marjoram

METHOD

Place all the diced vegetables and the whole garlic cloves on a greased baking tray. Drizzle with some olive oil, salt and pepper and shake to coat the veggies. Now roast hot and fast in an oven of 220C for about 20-30 minutes until the vegetables are roasted and delicious. This will depend on what size you cut them, so adjust your time as required.

MARINADE

Mix up all your marinade ingredients. Stir until the sugar has dissolved. Place your cooled roasted vegetables in sterilized jars and then top with this marinade. Store in the fridge and use over the next few weeks! Delicious on bruschetta on a base of cream cheese or ricotta.

Spring Pea Pasta Filling or Sauce

SERVINGS: 4-6

INGREDIENTS

2 cups frozen peas
1/2 cup parmesan cheese
1/2 cup ricotta cheese
2 tablespoons lemon zest
2 tablespoons fresh chopped mint
2 cloves crushed garlic
Zest of one lemon

METHOD

Combine all ingredients in a food processor and season to taste. Be careful to ensure the filling is not too wet; it should be a thick, dry, slightly rough paste.

Serve stirred through your choice of cooked pasta, with Burnt Butter Sauce or a dressing of Lemon Oil. Top with pea shoots or micro herbs, prosciutto bark and grated Parmigiana Reggiano.

BURNT BUTTER SAUCE

Simply brown 100g butter over low heat with fresh sage leaves, and use this gorgeous fragranced butter to drizzle and lift the flavour of the pasta. Add lemon/lime zest for a flavour sensation.

Pangritata (Crispy Breadcrumbs for Pasta)

SERVINGS: 4-6

INGREDIENTS

1/4 cup fresh white breadcrumbs,
1 clove minced garlic
4 tablespoons herbs like parsley, basil, thyme, oregano and sweet marjoram
zest of one lemon
Olive oil to fry

METHOD

Heat a frying to medium heat with the olive oil, add the breadcrumbs and remaining ingredients and toast lightly, stirring all the time and ensuring the crumbs don't burn.
You can serve it immediately on a wide range of dishes or allow it to cool and keep it in the freezer for the next time you need some gorgeous savoury crunch on a dish.

Easy Risotto's

Easy Risotto's

SERVINGS: 4-6

INGREDIENTS

50 ml Olive oil
1 onion, finely chopped
2 cloves garlic, finely chopped
1 cup Arborio rice
1 tablespoon parsley, chopped
1 tablespoon sage, chopped
80ml white wine (optional)
750ml hot mushroom, vegetable or chicken stock (this depends on the size of the pot you are using, and also don't make this stock too strong as it reduces and will leave you with salty rice!)

NOW CHOOSE YOUR FLAVOURS BY ADDING EITHER OF THESE:

1/2 cup fresh porcini mushrooms or 2 tablespoons dried, blended mushroom power
1/2 cup finely diced bacon
1/2 cup fresh peas and 2 tablespoons pesto
1/2 cup pumpkin mash
1 cup diced zucchini and 4 tablespoons bacon
OR ANYTHING YOUR HEART DESIRES

GARNISH

80g grated Parmesan or pecorino

METHOD

Chef Mel's NOTE: Risotto's are so versatile. You can literally make so many delicious flavours as you show off your newfound risotto-making skills. Always start with this base recipe, and then add YOUR favourite flavour for success every single time. Bellissimo!

Heat the olive oil in a medium frying pan or saucepan. Add the onion and garlic and cook, stirring, over gentle heat.
If you are adding bacon or sausage or similar, you can add it now to let it cook and brown up.
Add the rice and ensure that all grains are coated with the oil. Add the mushrooms, then whilst stirring, add the wine, and when absorbed, start adding the hot stock, 1 cup at a time, allowing it to be absorbed before more is added.
Now add your choice of flavour and the herbs of your choice, and then keep stirring it through.
Once your ingredients are cooked through, and the risotto is lovely and, silky and a little soupy, you can adjust your seasoning and add the cheese. Serve.
If you are awesome at stirring stuff, you are going to be great at making magnificent risotto.

Salse

Sauces

Easy Cheesy Sauce
For your Lasagne or other dishes

SERVINGS: 6-8

INGREDIENTS

125g butter
100 g plain flour
1 litre milk
200g grated cheddar or pecorino cheese
3 ml salt
ground pepper to taste

METHOD

Melt the butter in a large saucepan and then take off the heat.
Grab a whisk and whisk in all of the flour until it forms a smooth paste. This sexy little paste is called a 'roux'.
Once smooth, add the milk a little bit at a time, WHISKING so you incorporate the milk slowly. Don't go all in with the milk, as it will be difficult to get rid of the lumps. Slow and steady wins the race here.
Once nice and smooth, return to the heat and stir until this gorgeous silky sauce starts to boil and the flour has cooked through. It would help if you stirred pretty much the whole time, or else the bottom tends to burn. It only needs to boil once.

Once this has cooked through, remove from the heat and add the salt, pepper and cheese. Always taste your food and adjust the seasoning when necessary; it shows you care and will also make you more 'cheffy'.
The sauce should still be hot enough to melt that grated cheese. Never boil the sauce when the cheese is in; it will split.

Truffle or Porcini Cream Sauce

SERVINGS: 2-4

INGREDIENTS

2 tablespoons dried mushroom powder (food process dried mushrooms)
OR 1 cup finely minced mushroom
Half teaspoon salt *OR vegetable stock powder OR stock cube*
125 ml fresh cream
250 ml water
1 tablespoon truffle tapenade *OR 2 tablespoons truffle oil*

METHOD

Heat all these ingredients together over medium heat and then allow them to thicken to the required consistency. Always taste before you serve; if it's too thick and salty, add more cream or water; if it's too thin and not tasty enough, season with salt to taste.

Sexy Lemon Pepper Mayonnaise

MAKES JUST OVER 350ML

INGREDIENTS

1 egg yolk at room temperature (your egg MUST not be cold!!!)
3ml salt
5ml Dijon or grainy mustard
Pinch white pepper
20ml lemon juice
2 teaspoons lemon zest
1/2 teaspoon crushed black peppercorns
250 - 300 ml vegetable oil such as sunflower or canola, or rice bran (do not use olive oil)

METHOD

Blend the egg, salt, mustard, pepper and lemon juice/vinegar together first until nice and smooth; you can do this by hand or use a stick blender or mixer to help.

Once smooth, start adding 250- 300ml oil in a thin stream until the mixture starts to thicken; continue to pour until all the oil has been incorporated.

If you curdle the mix, simply add the curdled mix using the method above, but add it into a NEW egg mixture.

Sugo Sauce

SERVINGS: 4-6

INGREDIENTS

30 ml Olive oil to fry
1 onion finely chopped
2 cloves garlic
500-700ml tomato passata
Salt and pepper to season
1 pinch chilli flakes

METHOD

Fry the onions and the garlic in the oil until just soft.
Now add the tomato Passata/puree and the seasoning and cook through.
Simply place these gorgeous ingredients in a food processor or use a stick blender and blend until smooth. A fantastic accompaniment to a wide variety of dishes. I love to make extra, and then freeze for next time.

Sugo Sauce with Roasted Capsicum

SERVINGS: 4-6

INGREDIENTS

30 ml Olive oil to fry
1 onion finely chopped
2 cloves garlic
1 cup roasted red capsicums
(cut in half, place under the grill until the skin goes black, cool, and then remove skin)
500ml tomato passata
Salt and pepper to season
1 pinch chilli

METHOD

Fry the onions and the garlic in the oil until just soft.
Now add the cooked capsicum and the tomato passata/puree, and the seasoning and cook through.
Simply place these gorgeous ingredients in a food processor or use a stick blender and blend until smooth.
A fantastic accompaniment to a wide variety of dishes and salads, and heaps of fun to garnish with!

Sicilian Caponata Sauce

Sicilian Caponata Sauce

SERVINGS: 4-6

INGREDIENTS

30-50 ml Olive Oil
1 large zucchini
2 yellow squash
1 eggplant
1 red onion
1 stalk celery
2 cloves crushed garlic
1 large red capsicum
1 tin of cherry tomatoes (spend the extra to get cherry tomatoes as it makes a huge difference)
1/2 a cup of large capers in vinegar
2 tablespoons raisins (optional, but this is the true Sicilian Way)
2 tablespoons red wine vinegar

METHOD

Prepare all the vegetables by dicing them into large cubes. Everything should be the same size and shape for presentation and cooking time. Roast the diced eggplant in the oven, or in your air fryer, at 200 degrees for approximately 12- 20 mins until you achieve maximum caramelisation.

In a large, heavy-based saucepan, start to heat a large splash of olive oil. Add onion and celery and garlic. Add capsicum until starting to soften, then add the zucchini and squash. Be careful not to overcook these as they should be nice and golden but not too mushy. Add cooked eggplant, tomatoes, and vinegar, and season to taste. Reduce for about 15 minutes or until vegetables are cooked through but not too soft (they should still hold their shape) add vinegar and capers and season to taste.

Caponata can be served warm on its own or it makes a wonderful accompaniment to any fish or meat dish or simply on a slice of fresh bread.

Bacon & Porcini Mushroom Sauce

Bacon & Porcini Mushroom Sauce

SERVINGS: 4-6

INGREDIENTS

50 ml extra virgin olive oil
1 large onion finely chopped
2 rashers bacon, optional
4-6 cloves garlic, finely mashed or chopped
2-4 sprigs fresh thyme or oregano or marjoram
1/2 chicken stock cube crumbled/or use ½ teaspoon powder
200 g porcini or other mushroom, minced or thinly sliced/diced
100ml cream
100 ml water

METHOD

This sauce is perfect for pasta dishes, chicken dishes, steak or vegetables.
It can be made in advance or minutes before you need it.

Heat a large frying pan with the olive oil.
Add the garlic, onions and bacon and stir until nicely brown and cooked.
Add the mushrooms and the herbs and stir until cooked over a medium heat.
When all the ingredients are cooked and fragrant, add the stock powder or crumbled cube, the cream and the water.
Shake or stir and allow to simmer for 2-3 minutes.
Check the seasoning and then serve as desired.

Secondi

Mains

Beautiful Beef Ragu

Beautiful Beef Ragu

SERVINGS: 4-6

INGREDIENTS

3-5 tablespoons olive oil
1 kg chuck beef, finely diced
2 tablespoons beef stock powder
3 rashers bacon, finely chopped
2 large onions finely chopped
3-6 cloves garlic, depending on size and preference
200g sliced mushrooms
1 teaspoon Italian herbs like thyme, oregano or marjoram
3 tablespoons tomato paste
2 tins crushed tomatoes
400ml hot water

METHOD

Beef Ragu is an amazing addition to gnocchi or pasta or just on it's own. If you need this cooked faster, you will have to use a rump, sirloin, or fillet of beef instead of this slow cook option I have focused on in this recipe.

Heat and grease a large frying pan until very hot. Season the beef with the beef stock powder and then add to the hot pan and allow to brown; make sure you don't stir too much; the hotter the pan, the bigger the sizzle in the pan, and the better the browning will be.

Remove the beef and allow the pan to reheat; no need to clean it; we will use the lovely flavour left behind in the pan. Once nice and hot again, add the chopped bacon, allow it to brown, stirring from time to time, and then add the onions and the garlic and allow those to soften in the glorious bacon fat and olive oil.

Now add the beef back into the pan, add the remaining ingredients, and stir to combine. Lower the heat to a gentle sizzle and now allow to cook low and slow for at least 2-3 hours until the meat is delicious and tender. You may have to top up with a little water if the sauce gets too thick.

Now adjust the seasoning, and then you are ready to serve this amazing beef ragu.

Rustic Italian Gnocchi
with burnt sage butter & pancetta bark

SERVINGS: 4-6

INGREDIENTS

GNOCCHI

500g cooked, 'dry' potato mash
150g potato starch/plain flour
Pinch of salt

SAUCE AND GARNISH

80-100 g salted butter
12-18 sage leaves whole and fresh
80g Pancetta finely sliced and roasted until crispy (air fryer or oven) + Pecorino Cheese for garnish.

METHOD

Brush and wash the potatoes and then boil in salted water then whole, with the skin on, until tender. Never peel and dice the potatoes and then cook them; they will be far too wet to make a successful and stress-free gnocchi dough. You can also opt to bake the potatoes until the are tender. Drain, peel, and then mash while hot. I prefer to use a potato ricer, a fantastic investment and will save you heaps of time.

Add the flour and the salt, and then mix to form a firm dough. Place on a floured surface and knead for about a minute to form a soft, pliable dough. Do not over-knead; add extra potato starch if potatoes are wet.

Flour a work surface and then roll about a handful of gnocchi dough into a long cylinder. Cut with a palette or butter knife into tiny 'balls', about a teaspoonful size. Shape with a gnocchi paddle/fork if required, or simply leave it in a rustic shape. Boil in salted water until they rise to the surface, about 3-5 minutes. Grab them out with a slotted spoon as they rise. Drain, drizzle with a little oil to stop them sticking, shake to coat. In a pan, heat the butter and the sage. When the butter starts to bubble and the white foam has turned golden and smells nutty and fragrant, you can remove it from the heat and serve it over your gnocchi.
If your gnocchi has gone cold, use the same pan, heat it and add the gnocchi; shake to heat and brown a little of the butter sauce, but NEVER stir with a spoon. You can then add the remaining butter, shake to coat, and serve. Serve with fresh micro herbs, pancetta, and grated pecorino cheese.

Scallopini with Lemon Caper Sauce

SERVINGS: 4

INGREDIENTS

4 boneless, skinless chicken breasts (or veal or pork cutlets)
Salt and pepper, to taste
1/2 cup plain flour
2 tablespoons olive oil

SAUCE
2 tablespoons butter
1/2 cup chicken stock well seasoned
50 ml white wine or dry vermouth
1/4 cup freshly squeezed lemon juice
1/4 cup capers, drained
1/4 cup chopped shallots or onion
1/4 cup chopped fresh parsley

METHOD

Flatten the chicken using a meat mallet or a rolling pin until they are nicely thin and even.
Season the chicken with salt and pepper on both sides.
Place the flour in a shallow dish and dredge each piece of chicken in the flour, shaking off any excess.
In a large frying pan, heat the olive oil and, add the chicken and cook for about 3-4 minutes on each side until golden brown and cooked through.
The cooking time may vary depending on the thickness of the meat. Remove the cooked chicken from the skillet and set it aside on a plate. Clean any crumbs left in the pan.
In the same pan, add the butter and allow to melt. Add the onions and allow to soften.

Add the chicken stock wine or vermouth and lemon juice. Scrape any browned bits from the bottom of the pan for added flavour. Let the liquid reduce slightly for about 5 minutes until it is almost reduced by half.
Stir in the capers. Season to taste.
Plate the chicken and then drizzle with the delicious sauce.
Sprinkle chopped parsley over the chicken and sauce. Serve the chicken scallopini with your choice of side dishes, such as pasta, rice, or vegetables.
Enjoy! You can adapt this recipe for veal or pork by following the same steps with the veal or pork.

Involtini De Melanzane

SERVINGS: 4

INGREDIENTS

1-2 large eggplants
Zest one lemon OR half a teaspoon of pepper
Mix to make a smooth paste
2 cups sugo sauce (recipe in this book)
1 cup grated mozzarella cheese
Pecorino or Parmesan cheese to garnish

METHOD

1-2 large eggplants cut on a mandolin or by hand into less than 1 cm thick lengthways slices, place on a large roasting tray, drizzle with oil, season with salt and pepper and then place in a preheated oven of 220 C with grill on in the middle of the oven and then pop on the grill for about 5 minutes to really get some heat and colour into these.

Once brown on the one side (just watch these; each oven is different, so you must just wait until they are gorgeous and brown), then turn over and do the other side. Remove from oven and allow to cool.
Now mix your house-made or 1 x tub of ricotta with the following to make a smooth paste:
- Zest of one lemon
- Half a teaspoon of pepper

TO ASSEMBLE

Place a roasted strip of eggplant on your board or work surface. Scoop one tablespoon of ricotta and one tablespoon of cheese onto the strip and then roll up to form a lovely little scroll.
Place in a greased baking dish.
Continue until all of the eggplant has been rolled up, and then surround the scrolls of eggplant with spoons of the Sugo sauce. Top with the grated cheese, and then bake for 20 minutes at 200 C until gorgeous.
Serve hot or cold, with a little Pecorino or Parmesan as seasoning.

Chicken Involtini

SERVINGS: 4-6

INGREDIENTS

INVOLTINI

500-600g chicken breast fillets

12 thinly shaved slices of Prosciutto or streaky bacon

salt and pepper to season

80g sliced or grated mozzarella cheese

24 fresh basil leaves or use pesto

100g diced bacon or sun-dried tomatoes

QUICK SAUCE

700g jar passata

2 cloves garlic crushed

5 ml salt

large pinch of black pepper

fresh cherry tomatoes

METHOD

Take each chicken breast and cut it in half lengthways, then open the breast up. Bash with a meat mallet or rolling pin to make sure the breast is tenderised and, lovely, and thin. Season well with salt and pepper. Now place 3 slices of the streaky bacon or prosciutto down on your chopping board.

Then top with the thin chicken breast, sliced or grated cheese, the basil leaves or pesto, and some of the diced bacon or sun-dried tomatoes. You can choose any toppings and mix and match whatever you have, such as olives or blue cheese.

Carefully roll it up to make a parcel. Place in a greased oven dish and finish this same procedure with the remaining chicken breasts. You can choose between our Quick Sauce or Sugo Sauce (recipe page 44)

Pour your chosen Sauce around the base of the rolled chicken involtinis. Add a few cherry tomatoes around the dish and season by adding the salt, pepper and garlic and stir through.

Drizzle in some lovely, fresh, extra virgin olive oil and then bake in a hot oven of approximately 200 for 25-30 minutes until the bacon/prosciutto is brown and delicious and the chicken has cooked through.

Adjust the seasoning of the sauce and then serve.

Epic Meatballs in Sugo Sauce

Epic Meatballs in Sugo Sauce

SERVINGS: 4-6

INGREDIENTS

1 kg lean beef mince
1/2 cup grated parmesan or pecorino cheese
2 eggs
1 teaspoon salt or stock powder
1 cup dried or fresh breadcrumbs
1 teaspoon dried or 3 teaspoons fresh basil, oregano and marjoram.
1/2 bunch parsley chopped
1 batch Sugo Sauce Page 44

METHOD

Put everything in a large bowl.
Mix to combine all ingredients.
Shape into small to medium meatballs, and compact nicely with your hands.
Store in the fridge OR cook in a greased, heated, non-stick pan for a few minutes on each side until brown.
NOW ADD THE SUGO SAUCE, as mentioned on the page.
Turn the heat down and allow to cook through for about 20 minutes.
Drizzle with EVO, lots of shaved or grated pecorino or Parmesan, and serve with spaghetti or pasta!

WARNING

These are the best, most delicious, most moist meatballs you will ever taste.
Serve with spaghetti or your favourite pasta.
Cheap too... It's a pleasure.

Glam Lasagne

SERVINGS: 6-8

INGREDIENTS

Cooking spray or little vegetable oil to grease your pan

1kg premium beef mince

1 large onion finely sliced

3-6 cloves garlic

3 tablespoons fresh oregano/thyme/marjoram or use 1 teaspoon dried Italian herb mix

1 carrot finely diced or grated

1 celery stalk finely grated

1 pinch nutmeg (very important!)

80ml milk (optional)

2-3 teaspoons beef stock powder or 2 stock cubes

1 tin chopped tomatoes

1 jar passata (500-700ml)

6-8 fresh or store-bought lasagna sheets

METHOD

To be honest, this is just a standard lasagna, BUT to make it more glam, I'm adding baby truss tomatoes to the top of the sauce during the baking to make it delicious, pretty, and bursting with flavour and personality. I will also use sexy, good-quality beef, as well as really good-quality cheese for the sauce...quality ingredients make for a quality lasagne.

Heat and grease a large pan until it is just about smoking hot. Now add the mince...we want the mince to sizzle when it hits the pan, and IT SHOULD SIZZLE nice and loud and sexy.

DO NOT STIR. I know you are worried about this burning, and you are also worried about lumps, but let the mince brown and seal on the first side you put down FIRST.

Let the pan heat up again, and THEN you can stir ever so slightly just to get some more mince onto the base of the pan. My favourite mince 'fluffer' is one of those cheap plastic-coated whisks you get at the supermarket that only have about 4 loops.
If you don't have one of those, use a strong plastic spoon or egg flip to break down the mince.

Once the mince is brown and fragrant and sexy ALL BY ITSELF, then and only then do you add the finely chopped onion and garlic. There should be enough oil out of the mince that you have rendered off during your amazing sizzle-cooking of the mince at a nice high heat. If not, add some olive oil.
You can stir as much as you like now, by the way; that mince is SEALED off.
Now add the herbs, milk, nutmeg, stock powder, grated/diced carrot and seasoning and stir through. Amazing colour, isn't it?

Finally, add the chopped tomatoes, vegetables and passata, and you're practically done. Turn down the heat and let that all cook through, and then check the seasoning, and it's ready to serve.
This way of cooking will not only save you time, BUT it will add valuable flavour and vibrant personality to your otherwise boring mince.

Serve with fresh al dente spaghetti, shaved parmesan and lots of freshly chopped parsley.
Mel's Note: I love to get creative with my mince and change the spices, thus changing the flavour.

Crab & Prawn Lasagne

Crab & Prawn Lasagne with Prosciutto Prawn Bling

SERVINGS: 4-6

INGREDIENTS

4-8 fresh lasagne sheets
200g cooked crab meat mixed
with 400g cooked prawns
or cooked firm white fish (snapper or similar)

BÉCHAMEL SAUCE

3 tablespoons/50g butter
3 tablespoons/50g flour
600ml milk
80g parmesan or pecorino
¼ teaspoon turmeric /curry powder
3 tablespoons white wine (optional)
Salt and pepper

METHOD

BÉCHAMEL SAUCE

Melt the butter in a heavy-based saucepan.
Remove from heat. Add the flour and stir well to make a 'roux'.
Gradually stir in the milk, half a cup at a time, stirring continuously. When the mixture is smooth, return to the heat while stirring with a whisk. The mixture will thicken. Bring to a boil and cook through for about 1 minute, stirring constantly. Remove from heat, add the turmeric and season to taste. Stir in the grated cheese and the white wine – you want it to be ridiculously cheesy and decadent! Set sauce aside to cool.

LASANGE

Grease a baking dish. Place a layer of sauce, then lasagne sheets, then 1/3 crab/ prawn mix, and smother with the cheesy béchamel sauce. Repeat until all meat is used. Finish with a layer of lasagne sheets and sauce, and top with grated cheese.
Bake in a moderate oven (180°C) for about 30 minutes, until golden on top and pasta is cooked through.
Wrap 2-4 large tiger or banana prawns with 4 thin slices of Prosciutto; fry in a pan with a little olive oil; once the first side is brown, turn over and cook until the second side is done. Remove from the hot pan and then burn a lime that has been cut in half; cut side down into the pan until it has caramelised and is brown and juicy!

TO SERVE

For a round of applause, garnish a plate with balsamic glaze and black salt, and serve up the lasagne, top with the prosciutto prawn bling, petals, and black salt. Serve with a fresh salad of pear rocket and parmesan.

Polenta Bake with Italian Sausage

Polenta Bake with Italian Sausage

SERVINGS: 6-8

INGREDIENTS

POLENTA BASE

4 cups water

1 cup milk

100g butter

1 teaspoon salt

1 cup semolina

1 cup finely ground polenta

(use 2 cups of polenta if you prefer, and omit the semolina

TOPPING

3-4 Italian Sausage with fennel, chopped and diced

250 g ricotta

1 pinch nutmeg

1/2 cup cream, optional

freshly ground black pepper

1 cup cherry tomatoes, halved

1 cup cooked mushrooms or eggplant, diced

1 small zucchini sliced or diced

80g grated Pecorino or Parmesan

METHOD

POLENTA BASE

Place the water and the milk in a large saucepan with the salt and butter. Whisk in the dried polenta and semolina into the water, making sure you get rid of all the lumps.

Stir while bringing it to a boil over medium heat; make sure you don't leave this unattended for too long. It should cook in about 8-10 minutes if you use finely ground polenta; if not, reduce the heat and stir until the polenta is cooked. Pour into a large, greased baking dish.

TOPPING

Spread the ricotta and the nutmeg over the top of the polenta base, which has cooled slightly.

Top with the chopped sausage, cream, mushrooms or eggplant, and the zucchini and tomatoes. Top with the cream (optional), season with salt and pepper, and then bake for 25-35 minutes at 190 C until the sausage is cooked and delicious. Top with the cheese and serve with a side salad.

NOTE: If you have leftover baked polenta, you can cut it into thick slices, dust it in flour, and fry it like chips. Delicious!

Dolci

Desserts

Cannoli

SERVINGS: 6-8

INGREDIENTS

SHELLS	FILLING
1 cup plain flour	2 cups smooth ricotta
1 tablespoon sugar	5 ml vanilla paste
half an egg	zest of one lemon
1 tablespoon milk	1/4 cup icing mixture, sifted
30ml red or white wine	nuts or crushed chocolate
1 tablespoon vegetable oil	or chocolate curls to decorate

Use the other half of the egg to seal the edges, generally, you can water this down to make it easier and thinner to paint.

METHOD

To make the shell dough, simply place all the ingredients together and mix them together with a strong spoon until it comes together like a messy dough ball. Place on a floured surface, flour your hands and then knead to form a smooth, silky dough. It should take about three to five minutes of good, strong kneading.

Rest the dough for 5-10 minutes and then divide into two pieces. Roll each piece out, trying to keep it as a nice neat rectangle; you can either roll on your floured surface or use a pasta roller to get it nice and thin. Once the sheets have all been rolled and they are nice and thin, use a large circular cutter to make about 10cm rounds.

Have your vegetable oil ready to start frying; it must be hot enough to bubble as the dough hits but not so hot that it burns. Place the dough over the cannoli mould, seal with a little of the egg as per the demo and then seal, press and fry. You will have to hold down the cannoli to make sure all the dough is cooked. Remove from oil when lovely and golden, not too dark, and then drain on a paper towel and allow to cool. Once cool, mix all the filling ingredients together and place in a piping bag, pipe into cooled shells and then dip the ends in either crushed chocolate, chocolate curls, roasted almond nibs or pistachio roasted!

Enjoy!

Gelato

Gelato

SERVINGS: 8-12

INGREDIENTS

5ml vanilla bean paste
(You can add 100g chocolate chips to the hot liquid, OR you can add your choice of fruit or nut puree, and spices into the cold liquid BEFORE it boils)
600ml cream
600ml full cream milk
6 egg yolks
100g sugar

METHOD

Gelato is NOT difficult to make. But it is easiest and most efficient with an ice cream churn.

Boil the cream and milk with the vanilla, taking care to stir while it comes to a boil. Once boiled, remove from heat and allow to cool slightly. Adding lavender or cinnamon to the cold milk at the beginning means that the flavours will infuse by the time the milk and cream have boiled.

Whisk the egg yolks and sugar in a mixer with the whisk attachment (or by hand whisk) until pale, light, and fluffy. Now, pour the boiled cream and milk into the egg mixture. If the liquid is still very hot, pour from a distance or add a bit of the hot liquid to the eggs, stirring all the time, to temper the eggs.
Once combined, strain into a heat-proof bowl. Place the bowl over a double boiler and then stir until the mixture becomes warm; take care not to let this boil, or it will be a disaster.

Once the 'custard' heats and thickens, and you can draw a line on the back of the spoon without it bleeding back, remove it from the heat. Allow to cool, chill the mixture down in the fridge or even freezer, and then churn in an ice cream machine OR place in a suitable freezer dish and whisk up with a beater every 30 or so minutes to ensure this stays creamy.

Once set and creamy, you can freeze until required.

Vanilla Semi-Freddo

SERVINGS: 6-8

INGREDIENTS

600ml cream, whipped
4 eggs, room temperature
1 teaspoon vanilla
100g sugar

METHOD

Beat the eggs, vanilla and sugar together until light and fluffy. Fold into the whipped cream. Place in a freezer-proof container and freeze until firm.

VARIATIONS

Swirl 100g melted chocolate or 100ml of fruit puree through the mixture before freezing. Top with chocolate curls, petals or other bling of your choice.

TO SERVE

Use an ice-cream scoop dipped in hot water to get perfect ice-cream balls every time. Bling your balls with our dessert dust or simply roll in fresh petals and cookie or cake crumbs as per the demo.

Easy Vanilla Panna Cotta

SERVINGS: 4

INGREDIENTS

400ml cream
100ml milk
60g white sugar or use honey or maple, or sweetener
2 sheets gold strength leaf gelatine
5 ml vanilla paste or extract

METHOD

Heat the cream, milk, vanilla, and sugar to the boil. Remove from heat and allow to cool slightly. It is essential that you boil the cream/milk mixture at least once because it really does change the flavour, and panna cotta means cooked cream in Italian.

Soak the gelatine in cold water for no more than 1 minute. Remove from water and squeeze. Now, stir into the warm milk and cream; the mixture should be hot enough to dissolve the gelatine. Strain this mixture if you have added any other flavourings or fruit pulps in future batches.

Pour the cream mixture into greased dariole moulds or ungreased glass jars, allow it to come to room temperature, and refrigerate until ready to serve. Best chilled for 6 hours or overnight to allow the gelatine to set.

TO SERVE

You can serve these with anything your heart desires. In this photo, I have used a praline, but I use shaved chocolate, crushed cookies, crushed meringues, and diced fruit.

Chef Mel's Panna Cotta Variations

Panna Cotta is so versatile.
You can change the flavour as many times as you like.
Try these variations for years of panna cotta fun!

COFFEE PANNA COTTA

Omit 100 ml of the cream and replace it with 100 ml strong coffee instead.

CHOCOLATE PANNA COTTA

Add 50g melted chocolate and 1 tablespoon cocoa to the recipe, no need to adjust the liquids here as the chocolate will set beautifully.

LEMON MERINGUE PANNA COTTA

Omit 50ml of cream and add 50ml of strained lemon juice AFTER you have boiled the cream and milk in the standard recipe. You will only add the lemon juice after you have boiled the mixture. Then add the lemon juice and the bloomed gelatine; you can also pipe the panna cotta once it has set with meringue and blow torch it to make a lemon meringue panna cotta...it's the BEST!

BERRY PANNA COTTA

Omit 100 ml of the cream in the recipe and replace it with 100ml strained berry puree of your choice, then follow the recipe as normal.

BOOZY PANNA COTTA

Omit 50-100 ml of the cream in the standard recipe and then replace it with whisky, rum, and creamy liquor of your choice and follow the standard method and recipe.

Pear & Ricotta Tarts

Pear & Ricotta Tarts

SERVINGS: 6-8

INGREDIENTS

TART SHELL

1 ½ cups / 180g plain flour
60g almond meal, toasted
½ cup / 110g sugar
140g cold butter, chopped
Zest of 1 Orange

FILLING

500g ricotta
100ml cream
80g sugar
1 teaspoon vanilla paste
Zest of 1 orange
4 egg yolks
1-2 pears, sliced thin

METHOD

Place all tart shell ingredients in a food processor and combine until the mixture comes together. Cover with cling film and refrigerate for 30 minutes.

Press pastry into tart cases and trim. Bake in a moderate oven (170°C) for 10 minutes until just slightly browned. Remove from oven and allow to cool.

FILLING

Simply mix the ricotta and the cream together until smooth; now add the vanilla, sugar, yolks, and zest and mix until smooth and well combined. Once the tart shells are cooked and cooled, you can spoon them in and then top them with sliced pear. Bake again for about 8-12 minutes until the ricotta is set, and then cool and serve.

CHEF'S NOTE:

You can use a large tart case with this recipe. Your cooking times will vary.

Death by Chocolate Tiramisu

Death by Chocolate Tiramisu

SERVINGS: 6-8

INGREDIENTS

TIRAMISU CREAM

2 Eggs, separated
50 grams sugar + 50 grams sugar
5ml vanilla bean paste or extract
250 grams Mascarpone Cheese
1 tablespoon cocoa powder for dusting

LIQUID TO SOAK BISCUITS

50 grams Milk or dark chocolate, chopped
40ml of double-shot Espresso Coffee
40ml fresh milk
8-10 sponge finger biscuits

METHOD

Whisk the egg yolk with 50g sugar until lovely and, light, pale, and fluffy. It takes about 3-4 minutes; scrape down the sides when you need to. Now add the mascarpone and then vanilla and whisk until the mixture forms a smooth batter.

Next, whisk the egg whites with the other 50g sugar until soft peaks. Fold the egg whites mix into your mascarpone mix.

Make a mixture of the chopped chocolate, espresso coffee and milk and heat in a saucepan or in the microwave just until the chocolate has melted and the mixture is smooth.

Soak the biscuits in this mixture. It will take longer than if you just dip these in coffee, but the end result is worth it.

Once you have checked the biscuits have soaked the gorgeous coffee mix right through, break them open and check. You can then start by placing a third of the mascarpone mix in a serving dish. Add half of the biscuits in a single layer, top with the second third of the mascarpone mix, use the remaining biscuits, and then cover in the last bit of the mascarpone mix. Use a sieve and dust the top of this dessert with the cocoa powder; don't use all of it if you don't have to, just enough to coat the top.

Refrigerate for at least 3 hours and then serve.
You can keep this for up to three days.

Nonna's Sponge Cake

SERVINGS: 6-8

INGREDIENTS

3 Eggs, separated. Room temperature is a must!
½ cup white sugar
5ml vanilla bean paste or extract
2/3 cup cornflour
1/4 cup plain flour
1 teaspoon baking powder

TO SERVE

Whip 600ml cream with 2 tablespoons icing sugar and 1 teaspoon vanilla

DECORATIONS

2 cups strawberries, hulls removed for the inside and sliced
leaving some whole strawberries for the top
1 tablespoon icing mixture to dust

METHOD

Beat the egg whites in a clean bowl in your stand mixer until soft peaks form.
Add the sugar, a tablespoon at a time, while continuing to beat on high, until stiff peaks form and the egg whites are glossy.

Reduce the speed and add the yolks and vanilla, and beat until combined.

Sift the dry ingredients and then add to the egg mixture; fold gently using a metal or plastic spoon or spatula. It is VERY important that you fold but do not stir. You need to keep as much of the air incorporated as possible.

Grease and flour a 25-30cm sponge cake tin and then pour the mixture into the tin.

Bake at 180C for approximately 30 minutes, checking with a skewer to see if it comes out clean with no raw mixture.

Allow it to cool, and then loosen from the tin and turn it out onto a wire rack.
Slice in half, horizontally through the middle, and layer with fresh cream and strawberries.
Dust with icing mixture and serve.

Almond Biscuits

SERVINGS: 10-12

INGREDIENTS

500g Almond meal
500g Caster Sugar
5 egg whites
5 ml almond extract
5 ml vanilla extract
3-4 tablespoons Icing sugar to sprinkle

METHOD

Place the almond meal in a large bowl.

Beat the egg whites and essences in a stand mixer with a whisk attachment until soft peaks are formed. Keep the mixer running and add the sugar, a little at a time, until the eggs are glossy and the sugar has dissolved.

Fold the stiff egg whites and sugar gently into the almond meal and sugar to form a dough.

Use a tablespoon of dough and roll it into oval shapes. You can shape it into an 'S' shape or press it flat. Sprinkle with the icing sugar and then bake at 180C for 15 minutes, until they are brown and golden.

Allow to cool, and then serve...

Raisin & Nut Biscotti

Raisin & Nut Biscotti

SERVINGS: 6-8

INGREDIENTS

3 eggs, room temperature
250 g castor sugar
500g plain flour
3 teaspoons baking powder
125 ml olive oil or melted butter
125 ml milk
zest of one lemon
5 ml vanilla extract
125 g whole almonds
80 g raisins
4 tablespoons white sugar to dredge just before baking

METHOD

Beat the room-temperature eggs, sugar, vanilla and lemon zest together in a stand mixer until pale and fluffy.
Add the oil, milk and the remaining ingredients at a slow speed OR stir in by hand, forming a lovely dough.

Line a large baking tray with baking paper and then split the dough into three or four parts. Roll each dough part into a firm ball, and then roll out into a long cylinder. Place onto the baking sheet and then press flat. Dredge with some of the white sugar and then repeat with the other pieces.

Bake at 190 C for about 15 minutes until brown and cooked. Remove from the oven when a lovely brown crust has formed, and then allow to cool completely.

Store for at least a day before you cut these into thick slices, with a bread knife, of about 2cm thick. Place them onto a baking tray and pop them into a preheated oven of about 80 C for a few hours until they have dried out nicely and the cut side is golden. Overnight is possible at a lower temperature of 50-60C

Allow to cool and then store.

Limoncello

Limoncello

SERVINGS: 25

INGREDIENTS

1 bottle of vodka or grappa (white spirits)
Juice and only zests of 3 lemons
2 cups white sugar
2 cups water

METHOD

Wash the lemons well. Remove the zests, leaving behind any of the white, as this will make your liquor bitter. A vegetable peeler or zester works well.

Place the lemon juice, sugar and water in a saucepan and bring to a boil. Allow to boil for 5 minutes on medium heat and then allow to cool.

Add the zests and the vodka/grappa to this lemon syrup, and then store in a large jar in a cool, dark place for two to three weeks.

Strain and then pour into a sterilized bottle.

Store in the FREEZER; it will not freeze because of the alcohol and is best served chilled.

Enjoy responsibly xxx

NOTES

NOTES

Meet Chef Mel
THE HAPPY CHEF

PASSIONATE FOODIE, AUTHOR, ENTREPRENEUR, COOKING SCHOOL TEACHER, ATHLETE, CULTURAL GASTRONOMER AND CHEF

With a smile that can light up a room, she has been dubbed "The Happy Chef" by her students. Chef Mel is brilliant at making everyday dishes dazzling.
Her clever approach to cooking and teaching focuses on making recipes easy to understand, with time spent on excellent presentation skills.

The enthusiastic, entertaining, award-winning African-Australian chef and cooking school owner says that with a little know-how, anyone can plate up spectacular spreads like those you would expect to see in five-star restaurants.
Her intoxicating enthusiasm, authenticity and culinary lingo will have you hungry to flex your muscles in the kitchen.

She promises that this book will teach you some seriously cheffy skills so that you will be so much more confident and happy in your kitchen.

She can't wait to help you become the foodie you have always wanted to be!

Get ready to make delicious discoveries!

www.ingramcontent.com/pod-product-compliance
Lightning Source LLC
Chambersburg PA
CBHW061802290426
44109CB00030B/2923